THE
RESTLESS WATER

Poems By

HARRIET DOAR

ACKNOWLEDGEMENTS

Some of these poems have been published in *Southern Poetry Review, Appalachian Harvest, Cold Mountain Review, Logos, Aim* and the *N.C. Folklore Journal*; in *The Charlotte Observer, The Christian Science Monitor* and *The New York Times*; and in *Eleven Charlotte Poets* and *Contemporary Poetry of North Carolina*.

AN EYE PRESS FIRSTBOOK
From ST. ANDREWS PRESS
LAURINBURG, N.C.

PUBLISHED THROUGH THE GENEROSITY
OF
THE FORTNER FUND

ISBN # 0932662-47-1

Printed by
Bill Evans Co., Inc.

for my friends . . . wherever they
are, I hope this book finds them

CONTENTS

I.

II.

CONTENTS (Continued)

III.

IV.

I.

THE POOL

each in his element   but
                what is mine?
the snakebird coolly gliding under water
and squirrels
              fluid quicksilver from branches
flicker   like jays   the blue flash
             in the sun
weaves through the leaves   and clouds above them move
wind-drifting   towering   luminous   their sails
gathering light that glances off the trees'
leaf-tremble
          in the water   fishes arc
ripple   mobile   turned by braided currents
sun-shadowed   gray-green-brown   the hazel-eyed
in which I see a faint translucent image
the upside-down   the drowned   the inward sky
in which birds fly   leaves flicker   under water
troubled my self   what is your element?

STATEMENT

Soft and southern were the fall woods. The burred
Trees with leaves awry and the bent weeds blurred
And damply tangled, grayed and ran together;
No more distinctness of line than of color or weather.

Surprising, but unsurprised, across the road
A flexible yard of supple ripple flowed
In footless meter; paused, and raised from the ground
A sixth of its black rhythm, and looked around.
Unwavering, without fear or venom, self-contained
It measured its world and fastidiously disdained
What was not, like itself, precision without conceit,
Aware of itself, a comment: detached, free and complete.

THE GIFT

Now he has a cat's-eye to explore
The dark, the moth night beyond his door.
The shadow wings brush close, but he disdains
To shrink the shadows back into their skins
Or bend the shaft to probe for knuckled roots
That lurk to clutch the unenlightened foot
And pitch him on his face and claw his knees.
He is impatient with his yesterdays
That kept him rayed within the cabin's arc;
His frail light pulls him onward through the dark.
Alone, he moves beyond protected years
To lean an arrogant question on the stars.

FOREST FIRE

Hatred, bitter and burning,
blackened his fields and forests,
crowned in the tall firs,
blasted the least sapling.
Whatever could, fled;
all that was fastened died.

Deep in the hard ground
the buried seed expands,
struggles toward the sun
and life is blown in;
but the gaunt trunks stand
cursing the young green.

FAMILY HISTORY: FOOTNOTE

*'Life was pleasant in Rockport
in those days.' — John Hebert*

My brother-in-law, retired
gathered his family history
remembered   among the aunts and cousins
         second wives and speculations
that in his childhood
the family home still had a privy
         'well-made, multi-holed'
past the gooseberries, grapevines, summer kitchens, smoke-
     house, peach, apple, plum and cherry trees, rose garden,
     'next to the chickenyard and . . .near a large
     cluster of honeysuckle vines.'

Older than his father
         who liked to whistle
         played the mouth organ, sang
         'little songs in French, remembered from his
             childhood'
would ever be, he contemplates
that younger man, 'the embodiment of responsibility, honesty
     and good sense'
making an unhurried visit
'enjoying a little period of solitude . . . hearing
the buzzing of insects and the clucking of the chickens'

appends a footnote:
     1/ 'My friend Herb Wasson would tell me years
     later that the farmyards of his childhood in north-
     east Louisiana always smelled of honeysuckle and
     shit in the summertime . . . . .'

Grandpa, though, kindly and substantial
     (never scolded, spoiled his only daughter)
     had built his backhouse wisely on the hillside
     flushed water through a trough beneath, 'permitting
     the odor of honeysuckle to predominate'

Sixty years ago in Indiana.

NINETIETH BIRTHDAY

I remember Miss Sallie, who lived to be
a very old lady
amused at me
in the fading sunshine of late afternoon
drinking tea
that had been stirred with a thin coin spoon

a Bible on her knee
lace, and a velvet band around her throat

the wind in the old tree played a remote
tune for the ghostly leaves that turned in the sun

pinned
with a circle, garnets and small pearls
'of no value except the sentiment'
she remembered the girls
the apple-blossom girls
graceful in curls and cool white petticoats
and the young men riding debonair to their hunt

and smiled, watching me take my grave young notes

and saw the carriage, stopped on Tryon Street
as an empire crumbled   men stepped warily up to greet
Jefferson Davis, courtly, haggard of eye

irrelevancies
of the wind, irrelevancies

the leaves of the Bible and the leaves of the tree
were tipped with gold
I used to wonder what the dressed-up old
ladies found so amusing in life
                              and me.

THE JOY OF THE LORD
(Mattie's Conversion)

I woke up singing . . .
The sun was shouting
Everything was glittering
I'd been born.

Never thought about it
Till I lay in my bed
That was my first one
(I've got twelve)
I could hear music
Breathing through my nostrils
Music was breathing
Out of my head

No matter what
My lips were saying
Something inside of me
Kept right on
In my breast
Something kept saying
    Forgive me
    Forgive me
    Forgive me, Lord

I felt like a man
Had done a murder
Waiting for the sheriff
Scared of every knock
All my sins
Sat heavy on me
Little weak voice
Cried right in here

I didn't even know
What I was praying for
What have I done, Lord?
I kept on asking
What have I done, Lord?
The voice kept praying
    Forgive me
    Forgive me
    Forgive me, Lord

Then the Lord brought all
My sins up before me

Way back to when I
Talked back to my people
(Oughtn't to do that
After they raised you,
Almost died for you,
Oughtn't to do it)

Then the Lord took me up
Showed me all my relatives
Standing so far off
They looked like sparrows
I heard the hymns singing
I seen the angels
But that didn't cure me
Of my sins

Nothing would help me
Until I could say it
Say it and mean it:
    Thy will be done
Even if it's torment
Forever and ever
Send me to torment
    Thy will be done

Woke up in the morning
I woke up singing
The sun was shouting!
Everything was glittering!
I woke up in the morning
I'd been born!

Got to get along now
Got to get to High Point
Want to be shouting
Shouting tonight
Going to my daughter's
Get there by church time
I want to be shouting
Shouting tonight

(I woke up singing
Everything was glittering
The sun was shouting
I'd been born)

7

THE JUDGE'S WIDOW

She whose hair lies
Like blown snow
Above her blue eyes
About her child's face
Walks to and fro

Where violets grow
Beneath tall trees;
She does not bruise
The blue-eyed flowers
But as she passes
The tall trees, kisses
The rough bark.

In her walled park
She hurts no thing;
She touches only these
Deep-rooted ones, whose
Green hair is spring
Whose shade is summer.
They move and murmur
Softly above
And never startle.

She is as gentle.
Under the trees
Her face is smooth; she is
No more afraid.
Remember, when she dies,
Here she walked in love:
Bury her in shade.

Screen her from dread
Secure forever
Trees arching over
Green leaf or dead
Dead leaf or shadow . . .

She was their lover;
Leave her to their shade.

THREE TWILIGHTS

I.   Profile

Grandfather Mountain

Over this mountain of a lying-down man
the air is palest green
too thin
to hold up even this thin moon
which slides so smoothly, so irrevocably
down the smooth sky.

II.   Architecture

Blocks buildings and toy spires
that were important to the sun
crumble now into the night
while
stars grow out of the dark
Enormously.

III.   Incinerator

Butterflies of ash
lift papery and pale on the blue smoke's breath.
My thoughts, all day as aimless and as light,
seem for a moment, poised above their death,
beautiful and exultant in their flight.

RIVER POEM

Twilight
The meanings slip

Shift with the mist
The magic change of light

Slip like the minnows
Silvery, through the fingers

Pale, watery fingers
Closing on escape

NOSTALGIA FOR THE RIVER

I.   Evensong

white heron
motionless
fisher in green
twilight water
under an
apricot sky

II.   Lullaby

clouds
cover me
wind
cool me
trees
talk to me
rain
sing me to sleep

III.   What I Want to Do

is lie on the pier
in the sunshine
and slide
in the water
and swim
in the greenness
and drink
on the porch
barefooted
and listen to music
drowse
and make love
and eat shrimp
watch the water
grow dark and the moon
growing bright
in the sky
in the river
and sleep
in the shiver of moonlight
and wind

once again   11

OCTOBER

The green moon turns orange, a wrinkled persimmon
The possum drags its scaly tail through autumn
I stand here in the dark, aging too fast

TROPISM

I think I'm
       migratory
and the sadness
that pulls at me
in autumn
is not the sadness
of death
but the urge
to go elsewhere

follow the sun
follow something

you,
perhaps

THIS FRIENDSHIP

this friendship, then,
is seed, not food,
a grain:

stem, leaf, and fruit
implicit
not revealed

as in the seed of God
a universe was sealed.

CATS AT TWILIGHT

All cats are gray in the dark

visible, secretive
hungry
they disappear at twilight
gray into gray
ghost into mist

materialize
at dawn
familiar, full, domestic
self-satisfied and round as rolls
set warm to rise

hearth-sleepers
baking slowly like good bread.

CRYSTALS

No two are alike:
Not snowflakes,
Not friends.

THE THORN

All of that spring is in one memory:
In tears, leaning against a window teared with rain
I looked at the rainblown, twisted whitethorn tree.
What childish shame, what childish depth of grief
I felt, I have forgotten, but not the shape of the leaf
Or the thin spine
Of the thorn scratching the pane.

WILD STRAWBERRIES

I am too tall
For the world of stems and grass-stalks, the small
World of the beetle's path, the ant's trail, and
      the bee's
Dusty flight; if I dropped to my knees
And parted the long grasses, would I ever find
The stem bent down
Under
Its tiny crown
Of red sweetness, hidden and wild,
Or did it grow only for the child
Who lived nearer the level of the ground,
The level of wonder?

I REMEMBER

I remember the buckled trunk in the attic, and everything
          in it
The wide black velvet hat banded with gold wheat
The yellowed wedding-lace and the tortoise-shell comb
The Christmas-angel costume from the Sunday-school
          pageant
With tinsel wings.

Everything had been something wonderful when it was new;
The flavor lingered in the fading colors
And in the spotted photographs and the broken jewelry
And in the packet of letters tied with rotting
Pinkish ribbon.

Ghosts of ghosts, we trailed the long dresses
Over the splintered boards.

CLOUDS

The great maned horses overhead
Are no bigger nor whiter than the dreams you have
(Now they are dragons out of the fairy tales).
There you are, and you think you are hidden by
      the grasses
That are not quiet tall enough. Someone will see you.
Someone will shout "Get up off that wet ground,
      you hear me?
That child hasn't got the sense God gave green apples!"

BUILD THEE MORE STATELY PRISONS, O MY SOUL

There are two or three things I resent about growing up.
Although it is nice to be in scale
With the furniture and the ceilings and the stairways
I feel much smaller in comparison with the stars.

I can go out without asking permission or even saying
        I'm going
But I can't take my dreams into the treetops any more
Nor a book into the attic and hide from everybody . . .
There are no attics any more.

And now that no one would stop me from eating the platter
        of fudge
Or locking myself into the bathroom and crying because
        nobody loves me
No one is impressed. It is too late. I am a big girl
And I have to curl my hair and shave my legs.

II.

CYPRESS GARDENS

Do not look down
Or drown, drown
Tangled in gray-green hair
Strangled in thick air.
In a dark sleep

Drift; drift deep
As deep
As trees lift high
Down to that deepest sky
Locked in
Obsidian

Traveler
Do not look down
Into that black mirror
Or drown, drown
Like those fantastic petals fiery in
Polished obsidian
Clouded with gray and green
Tangle of leaf and moss.

Do not listen to the drowsy voices
Of the enchanted birds
That haunt these waters
Or the slow-spoken words
That ghostly voices
Chant from the lost depths of these black waters.

Flower-bright eyes
And your white-flower face
Will float like living petals there
Deep in black glass
And your black hair
Twist with the gray-green tendrils of the moss.

Drift down
Enchanted sleeper
Deeper
Deeper
Drown . . .

Do not look down.

FADED TAPESTRY

She was locked in a tower; only the moon
Climbed to her casement, and with golden wand
Touched the straw spinning under her small hand.

She sang a song to the moon; if some tall man
Had passed the tower, he might have paused to hear
And loved her. But none passed. It thinned to air.

If she had died in singing, it had been
Better for her. It was the song that died.
A flower can bloom unseen but not a maid.

It was the song that died, and the desire
To sing. The sacred moon moved on to shine
Elsewhere. The fair gold turned to straw again.

FORTIETH BIRTHDAY

I dreamed that I had leaves for hair
That played in languor with the wind
Then all the leaves were turned to light
That burned upon the changing air
A violence came on the wind
The leaves were wild in disarray
They wept themselves in scarlet tears
That bled their glory all away

And I awoke in windy night
In dread to find my hair blown gray.

IN THE MORNING

In the morning the tranquil face
Looks out of the tranquil mirror,
At home in the accustomed place,
Firm-fleshed, disdaining terror.
Disdaining kinship with one
Who lay all night in bed,
Unbodied, silent, alone,
Learning to be dead.

AROUND THE BLOCK

Dark streets, or lighted streets; it does not matter.
Lighted windows behind which people must be
Happier than you. The stars burn fiercely
And move in orderly fashion; if one would shatter
That one would be you. But it does not matter.

Move down the street; speculate on the houses
Where the light turns on and off. It is pretense
To assume in light and dark no difference.
Darkness is kinder; light points to you, arouses
Fear in you. Speculate on the houses.

Memorize the night. Remember the lonely
Pattern of lighted window and dark; the print
Of barely moving leaves that the lamp has lent
To the wall; the austere stars that are only
A little farther than these. Remember them, lonely.

FRAGMENT

In what deep
Caverns of the mind are put away
Those thoughts that lie docile and hidden from
    the day,
Coming not even in dreams but in the twilight of
    half sleep?
Some unknown one is standing in the doorway
Watching. I hear the spoken name. I wait to hear
The extreme question, but it is not asked. My
    ribs shake
With the beating of my heart. I am awake
In the dark, learning again that nothing is there
Except myself, and the bed, and the austere
Abstract and balanced pattern the blinds make
On the wall. I hear the small gnawing, the feet
Scampering. They are friendly. They have not
    caused the quick beat.

I learn faster than the heart. Watching the
    barred light
I am tranquil, but the coward blood still quivers
    in the night.

CHRISTMAS EVE

Furious clouds shut out the sky
And violent winds have stripped the trees
Of all their fiery aureole
Leaving them, now that wind and cloud have gone,
Stark in the twilight, stretched toward curving peace.

Against the thin
Blown crystal of the sky, a dark
Archaic prayer.

The opening stars unloose a shower of light
The rays are tangled in the roots of trees
The stars are tangled in the reaching branches

And sang like angels all that darkest night.

WINGED THING

Quietly, quietly lie here
While the night spins a chrysalis
Where the fragility of wing
Expands within mysterious
Dark walls. The helpless, colorless thing,
Silkily glassed in by night
Drains dark of color, formlessness
Of shape and strength; it is its right
To grow in darkness to its length
Undisturbed in its implicit
Pattern to be made explicit
When it can astonish light
With the extravagance of flight.

AT THE WINDOW

She is aging and barren; the wind troubles her
With its bombardment of fertility;
The pollen swirls on its currents, seedwings whirl
From the swollen twigs of the thousand-budded tree;
The petals drift to earth, and the stirred air
Lifts the dandelion's parachute fluff;
The grass-seed sprouts in the gutters of the tall roof;
The catkins fall and scatter; the tough pod
Splits with a silky exodus.
                              She stands
Behind the thin protective sliver of pane
Shivered with the impact of the wind
And tears distort the showers of golden seed
Scattered and loosed abroad in mad delight
As the shattered husks drift weightless down to night.

SO ONE WAS SAVED

            . . . But there were all those others
Weighted with chains, whose hopes rusted with them,
Who scanned the round horizon for the thrust
Of the hero's lightning   but the clouds were clouds
The gulls were gulls and would not stretch to horses
Wild-thunder-winged. Their days wheeled blue and splendid
Toward hopelessness; at last they drooped resigned
To see the dragon's breath consume their skies.

They died of slow starvation. Dry and shrinking,
The flesh a hero's touch might have redeemed
Could now no longer tempt the dragon's claw.
He was not coming either: o betrayal's
Fidelity . . .
            Now even the seas ignore
Their unimportant bones upon the shore.

TOUCH

the restless water
shattered the glassy light and glittered
as with a phosphorescence of its own
not the cold moon's

I felt
that darkest ocean wind tangle my hair
and salt or sand
minute abrasive   ground against my skin

o share
the darkness of my night!
you do not need to take my hand
watch   where the wind and water touch

the thousand splintered shiverings of light

VENUS ANADYOMENE

Water upcurved and flung to me
This miracle of fine-ribbed shell,
An involute simplicity
Enclosing primal mystery;
I curl it in my hand to hear
Tides of silence lift and fall
Through the spiral of my ear
Echoing infinity.

CALYPSO

In the eighth year he left the goddess.
Toward the end, time crept
Slower than his endurance, although he wept
A little to leave her. But as for the deathless
One, it had been a handful of water, draining
Away before it could be drunk. She'd have
Not time but timeless forever to remember
How easily he could leave
Her for the death she might not share, learning
Again that goddesses may neither die nor weep,
Jealous of Penelope, who when she was no longer
Loved, might sleep.

BEACH CARNIVAL

The horses of the carrousel
    Go down and up and round and round
With bravely curving reins to quell
    The puppet prance, the static bound.

The music dwindles and betrays
    Each charger in arrested leap
While lifted ears and lidless eyes
    Are shrouded down for midnight sleep.

Shattering hoofs and surging crest
In dream assault their painted rest.

From chaos of tremendous dark
    Unbitted stallions of the sea
Arc on phosphorescent arc
    Loom up and foam relentlessly

Shoreward to the swirl and suck
    Of grinding shell and loosened sand
Violence curls and crests to break
    In deluge on the helpless strand.

Thundering laughter shakes the night:
The little horses whine in fright.

EMPTY LANDSCAPE

The seaweeds swirl green under the water
And the dunes grasses curl inland against the sky;
One day follows another westward with the wind,
Days sunripened to pale gold on wet blue.
I could cry for your absence; everything else
Is perfect: billowing clipper-spread of cloud, and
      shattering sea
Sun burning beyond the island, red as death.

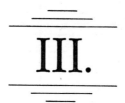

III.

SPRING, AND THE FIRST LEAVES OUT

Heart, you are fully as old as I am;
Be quiet,
Be more sedate.
Why must you keep playing tunes on the bones
     of my spine
Or skinning the cat
On the bars of my brain
For the sheer love of show-off?   Oh shame
There you plunge like a kite in the sky,
Quirking the gay, ragged tail
Of your haphazard joy
While I stumble along on your trail.

Silly acrobat,
You should be too mature for this idiot happiness;
For one thing, you make me ridiculous
And another, you'll wear yourself out
And, just when I need you the most, little
     brother,
Curl up for your long, dreamless rest.

DOVECOTE DAWN

Gray wings unfold above dark leaves
As pigeons spread and ruffle under shadowed eaves;
Cool dew-like voices lift
From iridescent throats; the quince clouds drift
Apart to show the splendor of the dawn.

The pigeons walk with coral feet on the cool
      dewy lawn.

MAGNOLIA SONG

The moonwhite flower
In midsummer night
Darkens and falls
The petals strike midnight
While the voice of the bird
Distills from denser shade
A clearer moonlight
Than the flower made.

SCREEN

On the still dusk
the still moth:
breath of silence, poised
for whisper of flight

THREE FOR AUTUMN

I. Turn of the Season

A few dry leaves
Fall imperceptible and light as dust
In a deserted house.

II. Nightfall

Where there is smoke there may be fire. The blue
Smoke of autumn is in the air tonight.
Tomorrow the leaves will begin to curl and kindle.

III. Dead Souls

Yesterday the leaves were blown in whirlpools,
Turning, like a flight of birds, all at one time.
Today a high fierce wind rattles them southward
And the smoke of forest fires is in the air.

RIGHT OF WAY

(Highway 54, Chapel Hill)

There they are by the roadside, dropped by the axe
        but still beautiful as their untouched brothers,
Greenyellow, flashing gold in the sun, or polished to
        a dull glow by the scattering rain;
Haloed and rayed with fire, their leaves will tarnish
        no quicker than the others . . .
But for these straight trunks and reaching branches,
        there will never be spring again.

AUTUMN CHANT

Trees are tipped with red
Red is the creeping weed
Scarlet and crimson hued
Stained and dipped and dyed
Color of bright blood
Color of closed eyelid

Autumn haunts the vein
Staining the flesh to shine
Translucent in the sun
Before the long windblown
Wintering dark comes down
O seal this passion in

AUTUMN CUP

In somber woods
the candles breathe
more bright than god's.
Translucent leaves
are stained with light
that sears the eye
cracks the brain:
shock of joy
pronged with pain.

Bitter communion
life with death:
drink from the wounded
side of earth.

WINTER SONG

. . . It is the migrant, singing in the rain
Outside my window. The last leaves are falling;
    branches vein
The sky like sea-fans. Sleek in black and white
    and gray,
Balanced on the bare stem, he loops fantastic
    color over a dull, disconsolate day.

STAR BOOK

Blue-white, and brilliant white,
Cream white; and yellow, lemon-pale
Or deep; flushed yellow or white;
Straw or topaz;
Golden or orange-colored; red-orange; and light
Red or bright;
Fiery red and emerald green together;
Sapphire or pale sapphire; lilac, rose,
And purplish-white; in this intenser weather
They burn the night

Of the mind; of the pages. They are a spell
Of colors. Tell them, beautiful and bright
And pulsing: the enchanted fires that haunt
Unmarked ellipses of imagined night.

A Field Book of Stars, Olcott. I counted 40 shades the author used
in description.

MEMORY

First the translucent reds, and then the yellows
And then the bronze-deep browns. Now there is only
Clutter of dead leaves rusted on black stem
And stripped silver trunks among the pines—
The anachronistic pines in ancient green
Studded with black cones and skeletoned
With black. A thin wash of rain is blurring
The green needles and soaking the dead leaves limp.

Life withdraws into itself, contracts
Into essential line. It is I who name it
Sorrowful, I who remember spring,
Cry summer's wreckage and the burnt-out fall.
Leaf memory does not mourn. It builds already
The many-layered bud seeded with death.

SNOW CHANGE

Moving through white
Fronds of unmoving coral
Swirling
Driftings of light
Undercloud currents
Whirling, unmoving the
White, unreal
Coral of this strange sea.

LAST WORDS

In this world there are no love and hate,
Only the dark pines and the bright stars
And the scent of hedgebloom in the night.

In this world there are no good and evil;
The mockingbird sings from the honeysuckle;
Song and flower lift out of the darkness.

In this world there are no life and death;
The blossom fills with moonlight, and the sweet
Petals are relinquished to the earth.

In this world light trembles into shadow:
From saturate air the song distills like dew.

SIX CHORUSES

I. CONSCIENCE

My eyes evade the mirror's light
To nullify its wrong and right
And I can silence in the clock
The argument of tick and tock.

But still I hear, I hear, I hear,
The beat of time within my ear
And the dark sight confronts again
A flawless mirror in the brain.

II. UNDER THE STAR

How many times, under this same star,
When the buds were swirling and breaking into a spray
Have I leaned back against this same rough pine
Melted in spring as the dull months dropped away.

The violets grow purple under my feet;
The night has taken their color, but sweet and wild,
Their fragrance softens the dark wind on my face
As it sweetened the earth for a wild, barefooted child.

III. NATURAL HISTORY

I have seen the glitter of a movement,
I have seen the cast skin fragile in the sun;
But the fluid life is out of it, it has vanished,
It left not even a print before it was gone.

Not even a bent grass to show direction . . .
Now we are lost between the sun and the shade,
Stricken not to be swift enough to follow
The evocation all too swift to evade.

IV. TWILIGHT

After the hot day, a small wind
Blew up from sunset, curling the tall trees;
On the telephone wires three birds sang:
A bar of black notes on apricot skies.

The heat stayed in, but I escaped
To walk in the bare grass with waking feet
And feel a cool delight start like the dew
Or the first stars shining freshly out.

V. CREATION

God gives us eyes to see the light
And eyelids for a private night
Whereon are traced, with subtle art,
The inward visions of the heart.

A lidless stare would slowly blind
The secret strivings of the mind
To formulate a mystery
Dark is the strict necessity.

VI. LATE IN AUGUST

I thought the butterfly was a falling leaf
Helpless and ghostly as a severed grief;
And so it was joy to see, at summer's end,
The papery wings tilt up on a frolic wind.

CROSSING THE BOUNDARIES

For a poet in jail

In your foreign country
where the trees are iron
what notations do you learn
what metal language?

In my world
softness of wind
picks up my hair
fingers the leaves
whispers of half-moons
shadows, water
clouds

How far you go from us
Who will translate you?

IV.

ISIS' SONG

Lie quietly, the dark is mine
Soon enough the day will come
Soon enough you will be gone
Who lie asleep within my arms

Lie whole and indivisible
Gathered up by dark and dream
Who will scatter heart and soul
On the daylight's flooded stream.

REQUIEM FOR A LOVER

I have buried you with the utmost ceremony,
I have covered you over with tenderness and care;
At your head a sutable monument celebrates you,
And it seems to me you can hardly be unaware

That it's rather indecent for you to wander about
The cemetery. It is something not often done
By ghosts with the best instincts. Come, read
    the inscription,
Smell the fragrance of fading flowers, and then
                        be gone.

I HOPE YOU CHOKE

When you stole my hate
I was a bee without a sting

When you stole my venom
I was a toothless snake

I did not turn into a silky flower
Or a cat to pet

Much good may it do you:
A fishbone in your throat.

UNTITLED

Surely
You are not afraid of me
I am weak and suppliant
I have woven this glittering garment
Myself, with my own hands
And I offer it on my knee
You will walk like the sun, wound
In a golden fire
It is beautiful, and

As cruel as desire.

Blackened corpse, twisted in agony
It was not
My malice that devoured you, but
Your own vanity.

THREE PERVERSE LOVE POEMS

I. Prayer

Forgive me
For the ugly word I said
And the cold eyes.

For the harsher word unsaid
Forgive me.   Pity my tears.   Love me

O my sweet lord

Do you not see the hairs rise
Like snakes upon my head?
Don't trust me:
I'd poison you if I dared.

II. Pride

I have braided this love and hate together
So well I cannot tell one strand from another
And have made so strong a coil, so supple and shining,
It will hang us both in its black and slender twining.

III. Love

This fruit has a tough rind
And bitter flesh
Be careful not to crush
The kernel, sweet and sound.

BALANCING OUT

One time you said to me,
"You don't give much, do you?"
I felt sorrowful
To have given so little.

You gave me too much:
Sleepless nights
Bitter thoughts
Pretense of not caring
Incurable wounds.

Maybe neither of us
Asked enough.

HAUNTED BY MOUNTAINS ON THE HORIZON

I thought about riding down that long road
Over the little mountains
I thought about you
And the two swerved together

     In my mind

We rode into the mountains and stopped at nightfall
In a cabin built out over a stone-chocked creek
That was a good night hearing the water
    stumbling through stones, and the stars singing above

Quarreling and making love in the moonlight
Why do I cry?
Why do you mutter curses?
Together we fall deep into separate dreams
Wake, sleep again   search, turn   tangled, untangled

Did we go on from there? together? in which direction?
In a gray shiver of dawn, the road dissolves
Did we stay there forever?
Someone turns in the doorway

No, one learns to leave, to drive on
Into this notched night
Accompanied by a ghost like a low moon

Over the hills the stars wheel, fierce and remote

THE NEWLY BLIND

September 1968

The blind, you said, are baffled
By snow. The snow muffles
Sound. Obliterates
Boundaries. A world
Unfelt, becomes unreadable.

This love
Fell down like snow
Around me. Where can I
Go? Where did I come from? *Where* . . .
Doorways
Are walled with quiet.
When I turn my head
There is no north, no east.
The snow fills in the footsteps of my past
And when I stretch
My hand, it touches nothing; emptiness
Curved back into the still
Snow
Silence, chill and ambiguous as your death.

REJECTION

All that winter 1 lay alone
Not exactly buried, merely dead

Leaves fell through my empty ribs
Nothing hurt. The sun dropped away

Wind tangled in the dry vines
Snow and starlight shifted through

      Cold and glittering
      Broken points of light

I waited for the weeds to bind me down
Tendrils cling, seedlings split my bones

Loose me in a green disintegration
Shape crumbling into damp mold

Nothing changed. My light and hollowed husk
Held stubborn, alien to the earth

      Body or shadow
      Rootless, itself, alone

I got up and walked away
You can't say resurrected
            but returned.

NOTES . . .

Ninetieth Birthday

When I first went to work there were still many survi-
vors of the Civil War and Reconstruction. "Miss Sallie"
is a composite of older women I interviewed as a young
and naive journalist; I wish now I had answers to the
questions I didn't know to ask.

The Joy of the Lord

The woman who introduced herself as Mattie came to
my door collecting small amounts of money for her
church and told me, over a cup of coffee, of her own
conversion. The moment she left I wrote down, as close-
ly as I could, her own words and rhythms. Shouting,
she explained, means "jumping up and down."

Special thanks to Ronald H. Bayes for a poet's
sensitive editing.

Proto by BRUCE ROBERTS

Harriet Doar was born in 1912 in Charlotte, where she
lives now. She attended Duke and later the University
of North Carolina in Chapel Hill. She retired after
years of newspaper work, the most recent as book editor
and editorial writer and columnist with *The Charlotte
Observer.* She has also been on the staff of *The Char-
lotte News* and of *The News and Observer* in Raleigh,
and has published articles and fiction in magazines. She
is a co-founder of the North Carolina Press Women and
in 1982 received a Samuel Talmadge Ragan Award from
St. Andrews College for contributions to the arts.